HOPE
THAT
HEALS

HOPE THAT HEALS

Reflections on a Life Journey

Betty Jane Clem

Copyright © 2020 by Betty Jane Clem.

Library of Congress Control Number: 2020921070
ISBN: Hardcover   978-1-6641-3868-1
              Softcover   978-1-6641-3867-4
              eBook   978-1-6641-3866-7

All rights reserved. No part of this book may be reproduced or transmitted in any form or by any means, electronic or mechanical, including photocopying, recording, or by any information storage and retrieval system, without permission in writing from the copyright owner.

Any people depicted in stock imagery provided by Getty Images are models, and such images are being used for illustrative purposes only.
Certain stock imagery © Getty Images.

Print information available on the last page.

Rev. date: 10/29/2020

To order additional copies of this book, contact:
Xlibris
844-714-8691
www.Xlibris.com
Orders@Xlibris.com
785734

Contents

Abstract ix
Acknowledgments xi

SET 1 SING A NEW SONG

Birds' Song 1
Angel Song 2
Infant Song 3
Bells' Song 4
Unfinished Symphonies 5

SET 2 IN THE GARDEN

Rooted 9
Rooted [continued] 10
The Heart Tree 11
Autumn in Mountain Meadows 12
The Gardeners 13
The Gardeners [continued] 14
Ebby's Adventure 15
Ode to a Beagle 16

SET 3 SELF-REVELATION

A Block of Wood 19
What Matters 20
Knowing 21
The Listener 22
The Listener [continued] 23
Love Does a Lot of Waiting 24
Tears Flow 25
Confrontation 26
Friends 27
Commitments 28
New Friend 29
Child Teacher 30
Recess 31
A Cleansing 32
Early Morning 33
First Guest Today 34
Forging Ahead 35
Survival Outside the Fold 36

SET 4 TO THE SEA

A Crane or A Crane? 39
Ocean's Sway 40
Rough Seas and High Winds 41
Rough Seas and High Winds [continued] 42
Changing Course 43
Rehoboth 44
Easter Eve 45
Tarpon Springs, Florida 46
Reflections on The Tidal Basin 47

SET 5 FOR THE FUN OF IT

The Bottom Line...51
Dreams Can Come True 52
The Blue Heron 53
Pelicans in Flight..54
Oops!..55
Oops!, [continued]...57

SET 6 SPIRITUAL STEPPING-STONES

Simplicity Beyond Sophistication, ...61
Ministerial Call...62
Unity through Hospitality..63
Unity through Hospitality [continued].............................64
Tree of Life...65
Ode to a Teacher 66

SET 7 ODDS AND ENDS

Fireflies 69
Team of Eight 70
Hands 71
Sunrise..72
Shaken Up 73
Shaken Up (continued) 74

SET 8 HEROES

Life in America: Before and After 911 77
Life in America: Before and After 911 78
Abandonment 79
Mr. Lincoln..80

Vietnam Veterans Memorial 81
David and Goliath 82
Prayer of an Itinerant Preacher 83

Epilogue 85
Research Bibliography 87
Historical Influence in Poetry's Development 91

Abstract

Hope that Heals: Reflections on a Life Journey is the first volume of poetry published by this writer. The contents include a variety of poems originally written contemporaneously to the poet's life, from age nine to the present. Subjects focus on people, travels, current issues of the period, and thoughts the writer recorded as reminders of her experiences. Looking back on years of diaries and journals, the author has selected entries featuring the theme of hope and healing revealed during times of joy, pain, discovery, challenge, and growth shared with family and friends.

Acknowledgments

Xlibris Publishing Corporation provides professional support to writers by writers. The structure of the corporation is such that each phase of publishing is covered by staff with expertise and skill in that phase. They diligently maintain contact with the writer and offer encouragement and solutions to the hurdles that naive new writers inevitably face. Had they not done so, this effort would have been put back on the shelf before it was completed. I am grateful for their availability and their willingness to offer support and guidance as needed.

To those who make dreams come true,
expecting, anticipating, and challenging,
with love and acceptance:
My companion, Sue Dickson
My late parents, Ruth S. and Raleigh A. Clem
My late brother and my sister-in-law, Samuel
H. Clem and Patsy Doome Clem
My brother and my sister-in-law, William J.
Clem II and Mary Lou Miller Clem
My extended family who became the village it took to raise me.
Teachers, who awoke in me the desire to read, write, learn, and think.
Faith and medical healers who kept my spirit
focused on seeking the greater good,
to walk a path of service,
who taught that intangible power and riches are found
in the spiritual, eternal promises of God.
My peers and friends, who pray for a more enlightened world
and have the courage to bring it into being.

Betty Jane Clem
Summer 2020
Fairfax, Virginia

SET 1

Sing a New Song

Birds' Song

From my porch

I hear them greet the morning.

High atop the sweet gum 'midst falling leaves

of the tulip poplar,

They flit about, catching the breeze,

announcing a new dawn.

Their song excites the spirit

and engages the senses

of all God's creation.

Angel Song

Seasons bring change in mood and song:
Birth to death, all life long.
Angels herald birth with joy and hope.
Jesus came down, ill will he'd cope.

Present through storms in sickness and health
Spirit breath blows in poverty or wealth.
Sing Alleluia! A song of praise,
Or a <u>Requiem</u>[1] toward eternity raise.

Come, join their hymn; give life to voice,
An angel choir calls to rejoice.
Sing this chorus with all your heart!
Help heaven's hosts God's love impart.

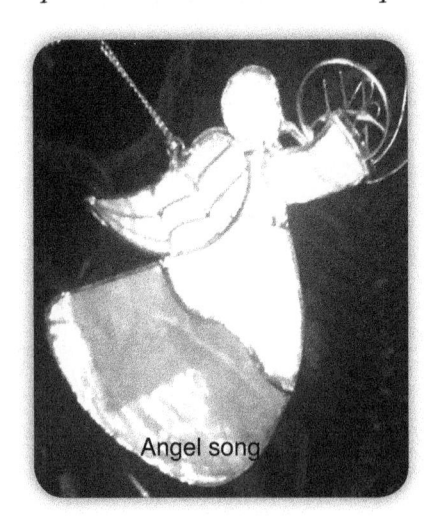

Angel song

---

[1] "Requiem" is a musical work written on the occasion of the death of the composer's father.

Infant Song

Signs of life from infant lungs:
a cry, a gasp, a rhythmic breath,
soon a grunt, a coo.

Eyes brighten, a smile appears;
tiny hands reach out
to feel beyond the womb.

Baby's first notes:
breathed from deep within,
the promise of life.

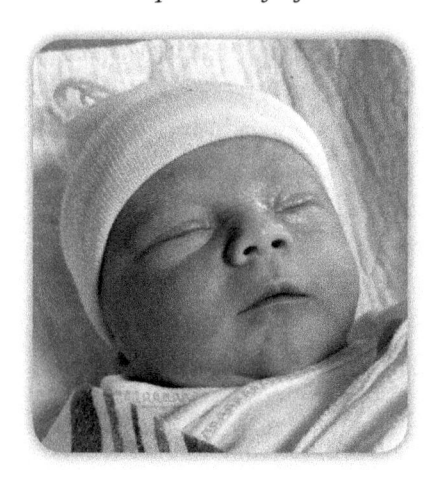

---

[2] Bryce is the author's great-grandnephew. Credit for photo is her grandnephew Rob Wilkerson, Bryce's dad.

Bells' Song

Each tune has a scale of notes,
Some low, some high,
A welcome sound to all within!
Sounds alert intruders nigh
intending harm to kith and kin.

Chimes in the wind delight the dogs.
Bronze bells attract them to a sleigh.
Dogs can't quite match the neigh.
Brass clangs aloud at the front door.
Can't say any bell's a bore!

Golden bells welcome snow,
Wood and crystal, each unique,
Porcelain graces a branch on the tree.
Copper enhances the cow's physique,
Silver bells peal from a balcony.

A steeple sounds a melodious ring.
Iron bells call the world to sing.
Each one crafted with artist's eye,
voiced with musician's ear.
Hearken to the beauty of the bells!

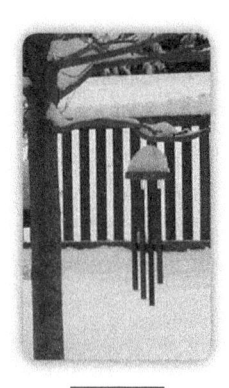

Unfinished Symphonies

The music stopped before the theme was through.

How lifelike!
An idea begun, interrupted, forgotten, gone.
A task planned, shared, judged, and changed.
A hope born, studied, developed, dashed.
A career entered, trained, risked, and diverted.

The music ceased before the song was sung.

SET 2

In the Garden

Rooted

Observe grand maples and cypress,
Standing guard at the border,
Grown old in years of sun and rain,
Pruned, fed, watched, and watered.

Rooted in earth's rich soil
Colors, textures, shapes appear,
Balancing a canopy that
Clears the air and cools with shade.

Branches stretch in all directions
Upward, outward, crossing over
As fine twigs bud in new forms,
Venture toward leaf and bloom.

At multiple points of intersection
nurturing elements await,
Morsels of ripening seeds and
a spring bird's first flight!

Rooted (continued)

Spring, summer, autumn,
Fresh green blades to fallen leaves,
Purple hyacinths and lemon daffodils,
Colors dress the border walls.

Winter brings a silhouette:
Bare limbs trace windy paths,
Ice and snow cast their burden
On the rose and tree alike.

This limb reaches toward sun's light
Spreads like the myrtle, arms aloft,
Finding food for stronger roots
And solid ground on which to stand.
And solid ground on which to stand.

The Heart Tree

On any given day,
after the fog rose from valley to mountain ridge,
The view from the office window became clear.

Across the Valley Road, o'er fence and meadow,
stood an aged tree as a sentry
for sheep and the village church next door.
At the tree's center, when in full leaf,
nature created open space
midway between trunk and crown.
The leafy frame for its empty space was heart-shaped.

Daily, the space inspired its witnesses.
Through it appeared hay fields, wildflowers,
the "Devil's Backbone" rock atop a mountain ridge and
expansive sky, where sun or moon hung for all to see.
The villagers' character, compassion and goodness
were tangibly visible in that old tree.

A lovely imprint on the rolling landscape
invited visitors to pause and pay attention to nature,
to stop and ponder the scene and claim the gift
from nature's heart to their own.

Across a road in a green field near you,
seek your inspiration in the hope to be found
in nature's Heart Tree.

Autumn in Mountain Meadows

*Morning fog teases the imagination
as darkness turns to dawn.
Clouds below our ridge-top refuge
lend a sense of "almost heaven"
as a windy front glides across the Shenandoah.
Time passes and clouds re-form.
Dewdrops cling to the banister
outside a windowed wall.
A lone dove's wake-up song
pierces the air with resolute tone
and welcomes the dawn.*

*Sammy Squirrel scampers o'er wet grass
Young jays' squawks echo in bouncing flight,
barely above a stand of maples;
red and orange amid green pines at forest's edge
join in praise for the new day.
Fresh
Reviving
Cool, clean
Mountain air;
October autumn day
and a panoramic view of
a West Virginia mountain range.*

The Gardeners

They went to the garden each evening after supper
to a place of peace and accomplishment.
Songbirds invited them to observe the sunset.
They watched tiny seeds pop through the earth
'til they took form as stalks of corn or vines of squash.
From their garden, they took gifts to destitute people
sheltered in a mission on the far side of town.

His was a bright spirit.
Neighbors heard him whistle while he worked.
Small children heard stories about earth's offerings,
and about who worked this patch before them.
His laughter, his joy, his grounded nature
took root in the garden.

Hers was a calm, quiet spirit,
forever supporting his efforts and
guiding the growing cycle in a Farmer's Almanac *way.*
She canned the beans and cooked the corn.
She shared with all who dropped by.
She said they liked her kitchen best.

The Gardeners [continued]

What is it about being a gardener?
Is it the excitement of seeing tiny objects mature
to become food for our bodies?
Is it the cycle of death and rebirth?
Is it sharing the fruit of our hands?
Is it partnering in God's creative order,
a channel for life, nurtured and borne anew
through each natural cycle?

The gardener is born in childhood as
dads and moms let their kids tag along,
dropping corn kernels into hills of soil.
The kids help hide the tiny seeds beneath the dirt
where they sleep until they change.

Finally, the gardener becomes the seed,
protected from exposure to life
until a light breaks through,
the darkness passes, and he or she is changed.[3]

---

[3] IMG 1433.pdf shows the beagles who enjoy watching humans work in their yard and garden.

Ebby's Adventure

*Stalking slowly across the lawn,
Ebby sniffs, listens, stares, and moves on.
She smells the soil.
She hears critters under the sod.
She focuses on a millipede
and passes it by.
She leaves the earthworm
for her feathered friends.*

*But grubs?
They are hers!
Appetizer, snack, dessert,
call it what you will.
She digs grass, dirt, rock, and root
to capture each crusty morsel.*

*Panting with joy,
she interrupts the mower
ready to return to her den
and rest.*

Ode to a Beagle

Woody stands on tiptoe
awaiting the blue jay's flight within his reach.
Watch him look and listen,
head cocked this way, then that,
prancing on hind legs as if he always stood upright.
Watch him reach with his nose
high as he can, up the cypress tree.
He dances the hunter's dance, quiet, patient, alert,
ready to pounce.

Lo, he waits in vain. Jay has flown far away,
never down to the tree's trunk, never close!
Woody turns away, leaving birds to nest and rest.
He hears another call,
a man–noise, from the opposite corner.

He races off to investigate.
Nose first, ears alert, tail wagging,
he catches only a chipmunk's scent.
Wearied from the empty chase, he pants back
home, excited by today's adventure
in the backyard.

SET 3

Self-Revelation

A Block of Wood

The room is stark and bare
save for a single block of wood.

Enter a lone, depressed soul.
The door shuts, and a voice speaks:
"When you say the magic words,
You may leave the room!
Find the piece of sandpaper and
go to work on that block of wood.
Whittle away at the rough surface."

Swish, swish; rub, rub.
Comfortable for now to be alone,
with a task that requires no thought
brings rhythm to the muddled mind.
The monotony slowly creates energy,
and a soul yells aloud for worthwhile activity,
"I'm sick and tired of being sick and tired!"

The magic words open the way to healing.
The seething inside is a yearning.
The energy rising with force is hidden power.
That awakened inner power opens outer doors.
Monotony morphs into positive action toward change.

As with the block of wood in the sculptor's hand,
the elegance inside is free to emerge.

What Matters

The ability to take care of you matters.
The relationship, the need to know
the threshold can be crossed, matters.

It isn't a matter of being unable.
It's that your self-interest has been
too long sacrificed.

You make too light of what you do,
Of who you are,
Of what is real in your life.

All else is blurred,
As if your vision had dissipated
And fine discernment turned limp.

Look again, at what is yours
to see and do and be.
Look up!
Affirm your survival.
Enjoy your rebirthing.
Claim what matters.

Knowing

"Your heart is visible in your face."
The speaker is a native Berber
from Rabat, Morocco, Africa
on the coast of the Mediterranean Sea.
In his home, we chat about his life.

Americans might say,
"Your eyes are the windows to your soul."
Both assure the listener of the speaker's trust.

We see beyond the surface to deep inside
if we know where to look!

The Listener

Week after week, clients enter a
simple, yellow room,
sit in a burgundy less-than-comfy chair,
beside a large rectangular coffee table
and stare at a golden carpet.

He sits opposite.
Sometimes he waits for the client to speak.
Other times he jumps right in
and leads through a series of thoughts
about experiences of life
and how life might feel just now.

Sometimes he describes his own day
or tells about someone who impressed him.
He's unafraid to wear pink or drive a Checker.

The Listener [continued]

He works hard, is soft-spoken,
Thinks broadly, understands others' feelings,
doesn't judge harshly,
finds humor in things humorous
and in people, but not at their expense.

He enjoys simple things:
the earth, people really into their lives.
He observes events clearly and gladly,
and engages people in sharing life.

An effective therapist must be so healthy
to know and care for people genuinely,
to enjoy all aspects of life and
to discern what gives personal joy.
Another's instability and burden
must not morph into his own.

The Listener hopes to be effective,
healthy and able to show others
a path to a whole, satisfying life.

Love Does a Lot of Waiting

She called, afraid and in pain.
She needed to talk.
Her life is in turmoil.
He is striking out
from different pain
he has created for himself.

He threatens to accuse and
destroy her friends.
The shock raises far-reaching questions,
"What if" questions that no one can answer.

Love does a lot of waiting.

Tears Flow

You asked her what made her sad.
She couldn't say.
It seemed a tiny water gate had been lifted
at the center of her heart
and the corner of her eyes
to let the tears flow.

You sat quietly by.
Then slowly, softly you spoke.
"Don't punish yourself for feeling the strain,
the difficulty of the process of
self-examination, change and
the threat of separation."

Confrontation

*When pain becomes too much,
we turn off our feelings.*

*When love gets too close,
we build a wall.*

*When we see our inadequacies,
we avoid dealing with them.*

*May God help us
to confront what is hard,
to be open to intimacy,
to face what is lacking,
that we may find victory
in our healing.*

Friends

Friends will become important again
in a new, adult way
sharing fun, hope, hurt, and fear
until grief subsides and
joy returns.

Friends are important.
Then life is bigger than we are.
We discover the value of the sharing,
the caring,
the knowing,
the walking
side by side.

Commitments

Life is pale without commitments.
Commitments call us forth
from isolation to connection,
from mediocrity to integrity,
from insecurity to confidence,
from despair to hope.

New Friend

You came, a stranger,
and you stayed.

We shared a common task,
'til one day
a moment on our path froze in time.

You cared to challenge.
You knew to correct.
You trusted to confront.

You stayed,
no more a stranger,
but a friend.

Child Teacher

Yellow bangs caress her face
and frame her lovely smile.
A single dimple kisses her upper cheek.
Budding artist, unintimidated,
she creates and gives her art away.

Love is like that.
Let us be innocent as little children[4]
'til our hearts become the gift.

---

[4] Holy Bible, New Revised Standard Version (Nashville: Thomas Nelson Publishers:, 1990) New Testament: Matthew 18:1–6; Mark 10:13-16; Luke 18:15–17 Jesus receives little children as he delivers the Sermon on the Mount, showing their innocent trust and love, unencumbered by adult fears and inhibitions.

Recess

Children play in the yard,
Yellow, brown, black, white
Scamper all around!
Swing and laugh
Scream and slide
Climb and jump
And run and hide.

Abandon inhibition!
Go free!
Let what's inside out!

Let that be me!

A Cleansing

We sit by a stream to be still,
To seek and to share,
Enveloped in silence.

Images enter our space:
The sounds of ripples
Water over rock, breeze over leaf
Cleansing us deep within.

To what great void have gone
Old wounds, late struggles,
and fresh pain?

Old scars relinquished,
New hope unleashed,
Searching souls blessed.

From that deep place
where the spirit lives
new birth springs.

Early Morning

*Awake to thoughts
circling within the vastness of mind,
Confined only by time and space
and the energy-drain of life's demands.*

*Faces are memories
and events, exercises
in the subconscious.*

*Reach for the surface,
Bumble through the crevices of half-sleep.
Here dawns a new day.*

*Dreams unfold
into the people and events
of today.*

First Guest Today

First thought upon waking,
A guest gently invades this day
With an undeniable presence.

None can know who, or where
The guest resides, save in the mind,
Suspended in buoyant abandon.

Spirit leads the heart to engage the mind
until all else must respond
to its pervasive presence.

Welcome to this inner space.
Stay awhile.
Please, stay!

Forging Ahead

*There are days when a question
becomes a crisis.
Relationships seem threatened
Jobs appear hanging
Growth is wanting*

*Strength is summoned
to withstand the question,
to firm friendships,
to infuse work with innovation
to stimulate growth.*

*That strength lies within, awaiting revelation,
to transform the crisis into opportunity.*

Survival Outside the Fold
A MODERN PSALM

Another day and nary a dollar,
It feels like time to run and holler,
What's it mean, this time apart,
When every sigh within the heart
is calmed by silent vigil?

It's right to be here, work does exist!
Grow new courage out of risk.
Suspend the angst in bold effort and trust.
Under any guise, new truth will rise
from the ashes of this fear.

Generous God, may the time be near,
Let the miracle of your grace appear.
Bring vision, frame space for survival.
Accept the surrender of a healing heart
for greater service apart.

SET 4

To The Sea

A Crane or A Crane?

Twelve floors above the ground towers a bright shape
Framed as a teeter-totter against the open sky,
Feet firmly set on the ground.
Tiny figures scurry about at its feet
guiding the load it lifts, making light their work.

Is it the graceful bird we call "crane"?
No. It's a steel machine!
Its long arm swings at the behest of a man in a cage.
Figures below are not sparrows,
But workmen guiding huge beams to their target.
A skyscraper is set.

Back at the stream in memory
a noble white bird on stilted legs
grabs a meal from the trout race
and slowly steps forward.
The ground beneath his feet cannot hold him.
Suddenly he lifts himself.
His arms are winged and his airspace limitless,
as he glides gracefully into the open sky.

Ocean's Sway

*The ocean is bright at daybreak
when birds and kites share common space.*

*The endless tide breaks our reverie.
Whitecaps break the foreboding blue gray;
Ships briefly break the horizon's line.
We are lulled into the mysterious restlessness
of the water's power.*

Nature lifts life and spirit!

*All returns to the vast rocking motion,
the ceaseless, swaying motion
of a calmer, rhythmic Sea.*

Rough Seas and High Winds

The sea is lovely, when all is calm and hospitable.
When the hurricane's eye threatens to make landfall,
warnings increase, instructions say "Evacuate,"
stores sell out of water, generators and plywood.
Convenience foods aren't so convenient!

The storm's aftermath is a sight to behold:
Homes washed or blown off their bases,
neighborhoods become jigsaw puzzles
with millions of pieces to reassemble.

"No known address" takes on new meaning.
The latest census of inhabitants is scrambled.
Phones are out of service; electricity, sporadic.
Lucky folks have a generator!
Few remain in place, at great risk;
others are happy to leave.

Rough Seas and High Winds [continued]

Animals seek higher ground for safety and an escape.
Beloved pets get lost in the chaos.
When the storm has passed, it isn't gone;
shelters fill with refugees.
An undefined period of rescue and recovery follows.

Citizens reestablish passages so help can enter.
Chainsaws quit, and neighbors find each other,
They identify the remains of their lives:
homes, sheds, stores, churches, and schools;
in some cases, family and friends.

Downed power lines are a present danger to survivors.
High water and floating debris threaten all.
As soon as local conditions allow,
Volunteers and professional caregivers go to work.
Rescuers measure loss in lives rather than possessions.

Rough waves and high winds rule the day for now
until the calm returns, the cleanup is done,
and a tranquil sea calls everyone home.

Changing Course

We walked to the sea, just a sister and me,
Sandpipers tiptoed o'er the sand,

A May breeze stirred, blowing mist everywhere
Sunshine's bright gold dressed the pier.

Sandcastles grew on the level below,
near the edge of the brine on the sand.

Kids played by the sea and my sister and me
as we watched every wave wash the land.

Take the bike trail along the boardwalk,
The breeze is warmer up there.

Stop for a while, chat with natives and smile,
Smell the salt and the fish in the air.

Like the blood flows on within our frame,
Water streams steadily, with might.

Life pulses our veins as the sea flows away
toward the vast space of Earth beyond sight.

Rehoboth

It's worth the day at Rehoboth Beach,
to feel the sea in your face,
to wiggle your toes in the sand,
see all the sights or sit on a bench
with a friend.

Planes overhead
sound their presence aloud
and we stop to look at the sky.
Sand feels as fine as the mist in the air.
Thoughts drift from still to free.

We see minimal water this side of the sea
and imagine a far eastern port.
Rising crescents of waves
Strike aloud on our shore
Ships sail from sight into lore.

Easter Eve

Easter Eve at Ocean City,
the moon shines large on the Atlantic.
The surf crashes against the shore
behind the Surf 'n' Sands.

The air is brisk
the sea is loud
the stars are bright.
Life is fresh
for celebration
and enlightenment!

Nature announces the power
of renewal.

Tarpon Springs, Florida

Greek settlers from the Mediterranean
brought their sponge-diving trade to America.
They found sponges on Florida's west coast,
and developed a factory beside the Gulf.
They built a shelter, and diving became
the lifeblood of a small town.
Processing the sponges provided jobs,
and this nation welcomed a unique culture to
Tarpon Springs, Florida.

Distinct fishing villages dot America's coast.
Small shops, cafes, and restaurants welcome visitors.
Pappa's Café looks out over the coast
where vessels cast anchor for the night.
Yachtsmen step ashore to refuel bodies and boats
Weather-wrinkled men spin tall tales of their travels —
Fish tales, pirate tales, night after night.
Tourists form lasting memories as they listen.

The food is good, the service, relaxed,
The aura, comfortable and warm.
The view is fantastic; crowd is fun.
Travelers applaud an evening well spent.

Reflections on the Tidal Basin[5]

The Basin is calm this evening hour,
yet reflects the rush of DC
Lights stream down across its face,
casting shadows of great men to see.
A band sounds forth, people laugh and shout,
traffic whizzes o'er the nearest bridge.
As jets arrive and depart our town,
their noise blends in with the rest.
Bass still ripple the mirror surface,
Claiming marine life in their path.
A world appears on the water's face
and dissolves in the paddleboats' wake.

---

[5] The Tidal Basin is a reservoir at the National Mall in the city of Washington DC, where the Potomac River and the Washington Channel converge.

SET 5
For the Fun of It

The Bottom Line

Who's the guy bent o'er the Slush machine,
Baring a crease we'd rather slight?
Folks rush past, cracking small grins
hoping to hide their delight.

Glancing back as they pass by,
Two young boys, in total glee,
Point with abandon at the sight.
Their giggles rise as they look back,
Clearly noting "That's his crack!"

Feigning discretion, hand over mouth,
Mom snickers, "Yes! That's for real!"
The man rises, pays for his drink
walks on, blind to his appeal.

Who can regret moments so real
that catch us off guard . . . or so we feel.
Who can forget the man or the boys,
or the source of their fun and joy?

People find fun in letting life be
spontaneous as a young boy's laugh.
That's the main point, the healing point
of people just being themselves.[6]

Dreams Can Come True

*Once upon a holiday, James drove his Jeep[6] to Macy's.
Arriving late afternoon, pressed for time and
parking scarce, he headed to the main entrance.
He stopped and opened the driver's door.
Once outside, he hit a spot on his key fob and waited.*

*Slowly, the Jeep's roof folded down,
The hood folded over and secured it.
The boot bent under the chassis.
The wheels raised into perfect curves
onto the undercarriage.
Once more, James touched the key fob.
He paused a moment.
He slipped the miniaturized, rectangular Jeep
into his hip pocket.
Nonchalantly, he walked into Macy's to shop
as astounded onlookers stared in awe.*

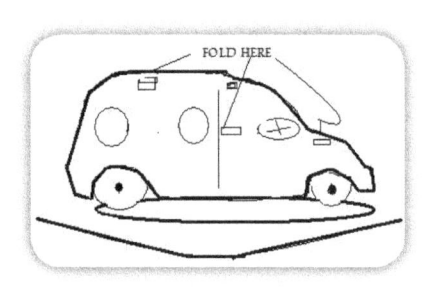

---

[6] Dreams beget stories to delight our wits and grow our imaginations.
   Years after this dream, an Israeli manufacturer created an electric fold-up car. It doesn't fit into one's pocket when folded. It does fit into a parking space with three other folded cars. Hold on to your dreams and make them come true!

The Blue Heron

Strutting across a meadow,
He gazes out at life.
Raceways and streams offer fish,
Grass hides him in safety.

He scrunches down to hide, in fear;
He raises his head as threats disappear.
He lifts his body to statue proud
and lowers his head to drowse.

Such grace he carries as he walks.
Such elegance seems his way.
He flies off in one swift move,
a memory long to stay.

Pelicans in Flight

A flock of pelicans approaches
as high as the seventh floor of the hotel.
We are in their space.
They pass by our intrusion
in strategic formation:
ten together, single file,
then in ranks of two,
and finally in their long-distance V,
always graceful, simply synchronized.

Imagine
their return to their fishing hole,
their migration destination
across the great blue sea.
They wave farewell,
and will return
after the winds warm again,
when the need arises.

Oops!

The rain persisted today.
The mall waffle shop served breakfast.
It was logical to go out to eat and check a few shops.

Some folks window-shopped as they passed by.
Others entered each store without buying anything.
Sellers were friendly, but buyers were killing time.

Older folk took that walk they need to keep limber.
Young moms brought their small children along
and hoped a skipped nap wouldn't make them cranky.

Mall security officers wished there'd be no incidents
to investigate, document and make arrests.
They took short breaks so they could eat dinner early.

Ms. Hasta Tuchit and Ms. Laffs Alot entered the anchor store.
They looked and compared quality and prices
with small business offerings up the hall.

They moseyed through the lingerie, purses, and gloves.
Prices were better at the mom-and-pop Shop
where they got great deals on reduced items.

They sauntered on to shoes, needing to sit *and look.*
They found styles that didn't suit their taste.
Hasta said to Laffs, "Let's check the socks and hose!"

*"Here they are," Hasta said, touching a display.
Slowly, trembling legs toppled from their perch
like dominoes set "just so," as if in a chorus line.*

*The noise of falling plastic caught Laffs's ears as
thirty dressed legs tumbled toward the aisle
tipping, spilling, and crashing to the floor below.*

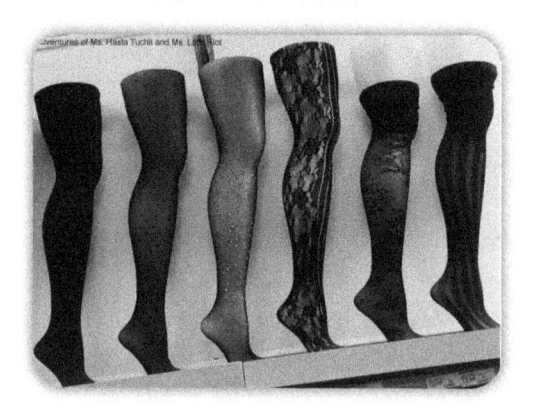

*Knowing it was near closing, the culprits left quickly.
Giggling, crossing their legs, and holding back tears,
with bowed heads they hoped to escape unnoticed.*

Oops!, [continued]

It was the day's greatest excitement!
No security officer stopped their rush to the car.
No clerk came looking for the perpetrators of chaos.

The two seniors looked back once, and relaxed.
They knew no one could identify them
as the cause of entropy and disorder.

"Wasn't that fun?" asked Hasta Tuchit.
"That display invited a customer response!"
"Oh, yeah," Laffs Alot replied. "Where do we go next?"

Laffs was in the car with her key in the ignition.
They agreed to go back to their cottage and nap.
This was enough adventure for one day!

SET 6

Spiritual Stepping-Stones

Simplicity Beyond Sophistication[7,8]
JUNE 3, 1982

Three red roses and baby's breath arrived
amid the stir of packing boxes, buzzing phones
and the busyness of moving.

Years ago today,
Three brothers' hands on her head,
The Church set her apart
"To take authority: to read the scriptures,
To administer the sacraments and preach the Word,"[7]
To be prophet, priest, pastor, and
Shepherd to a flock of God's people.

This day, as she leaves her final post
one friend remembers the pain of
unplanned departure and separation from her vows.

Three red roses and baby's breath:
A delicate touch to mark a delicate moment.

---

[7] "To take authority," from the Ordination Rite, United Methodist Book of Discipline, Cokesbury, 1968.

[8] Douglas V. Steere says of Thomas R. Kelly's focus in *A Testament of Devotion*, "An adequate life might be described as a life which has grasped intuitively the whole nature of things, and has seen and felt and refocused itself to this whole. The adequate life that Thomas Kelly had known he described with unusual simplicity and grace in the collection of his writings . . . Kelly called this life 'simplicity beyond sophistication'" (Steere, Harper & Row: *A Biographical Memoir*).

Ministerial Call

Mutual questions and common fears
bring us to a bound place
where firm hands, modest tears,
and gentle rebukes
call us to reassess:

Who are we
apart from our call to service?
What are we
apart from our call to personhood?
In what world do we live
apart from our call to humanity?

Let service be a source of strength and mystery,
not fully understood,
beyond our power to contain,
outside human control,
yet to claim and to enact
the greater call to serve God
and to care for our neighbor.

Unity through Hospitality

In the space between two persons
is a mutual need for hospitality.
In that gracious milieu, each is free to trust.

Each is open to the other.
Each finds the space adequate
to give and gain respect,
to listen to and speak truth,
to love and be loved,
to teach and to learn.

In the space between two faiths
is a mutual ground for hospitality.
On that ground, each community practices trust.

Each examines the other's truth.
Each looks for the other's purpose.
Find mutually valued words and symbols,
Exchange distinct cultures and rituals,
See shared family customs,
Hold dear their common goals.

Unity through Hospitality [continued]

*In the space between two races
is a mutual hope in hospitality.
In that precious hope, each finds strength.*

*Each owns a rich faith culture;
Each yearns to grow in mind and spirit,
Give smiles and tears for mutual benefit,
Own and share old stories, songs, and games
that reflect inherent courage
through struggle and self-realization.*

*In the space between two nations
is a mutual yen for hospitality.
In that yearning, each grows wiser.*

*Each hears the other's world view.
Each wants their young to be safe and well,
Claim mutually beneficial strengths,
Share visions and dreams,
Lift the value of freedom and commonality
to live together in a productive world.*

Tree of Life

Shabbat had just begun.
The intergenerational Jewish neighborhood
gathered for special services
at the Tree of Life Synagogue in Pittsburgh.
Families celebrated the spiritual identity of a child
born into a faith of ancient roots.

Into that sacred space came
an interloper carrying a fatal weapon,
intending to maim and kill
as many Jews as he could.

How have we lost our way?
How can free people equate pride for nation
with hatred for all who do not share a
common life view,
blinded by limits of nationality, race, and creed?
Would we rather live in hatred,
where greed for power
can only lead to emptiness and death?
The Tree of Life calls every Jew to a life of hope.
May the day never return when
hate's darkness overpowers hope's light
within the human family.

Ode to a Teacher

Stern for your small stature,
You stood before us with unquestioned authority.
The written page vibrated with your reading.
Drama was Life and Life, drama.
Your smile and your wise words
revealed your humanity.
Time passed.

I stood under the authority of the Church.
Scriptures read and prayers shared,
you came and knelt before the table.
You smiled.
It was humbling to serve you.

We were made equal only by the bread and wine,
The Body and Blood of Christ.
Drama is Life and Life, Drama.
The Lord of the Drama,
The Lord of Life
made us one.

SET 7
Odds and Ends

Fireflies

As night falls beyond dusk
Small creatures otherwise unnoticed
Begin their visible vigil in the yard.
Trees black against the darkening sky
Fill suddenly with magic, twinkling lights,
As if celebrating America's Fourth of July.

Glow, glimmer,
Lighten our world, our vision, and our thoughts.
Focus our imaginings 'til we make light
as lovely
as gentle,
as penetrating
as your glow!

Team of Eight

A team of eight
Wielding spades, shovels, and rakes
Edges the path behind the neighbor's yard.

Two dig the line with spades,
Two scoop debris with shovels.
End men rake away what the shovels missed.

Their task is complete at path's end and
the team moves on to the next one.

Satisfaction comes at day's end
in the sounds, the rhythms,
the movement and the rear view:
A clean, clear path for travelers' feet.

Hands

So much there is to hands!

Shades of color and texture,
Smooth or wrinkled, soft or calloused,
they tell of days of toil and caring.

Some fingers are long and lean.
Some are absent,
Others misshaped,
Feeling, reaching, projecting,
expressing love and need.

Life flows between hands
as fingers clasp together.
Hands entwined bring new life and sense.
Where one ends, the other begins.

The pulse of life and the miracle of union
are wrapped in joined hands.[9]

---

[9] IMG 1324.pdf is from Super Stock, and has been decreased in size to fit the poem.

Sunrise

Out the eastern window, day breaks,

The jet stream slices the gray space
between orange and pink.

Birds in flight draw the eye to their beauty.

From first bright orange on the horizon
to a brilliant disc above the black hillside,
orange overcomes gray.

Pink streaks stretch lavender fingers northward.
A single goose honks his greeting.
His voice soon becomes a chorus.

Black, bare trees are mere silhouettes
between the land and the light.
Willow branches brighten,
warmed by rays of gold.
They cast their shadow on the snow-clad lawn.
A winter sunrise.

Shaken Up

The day was dark, and predictably stormy.
Meteorologists called for snow.
Ominous clouds drew closer and denser.
Nature's eerie calm drew suspicion
from those outdoors.

People worked at their desks and stations.
The writer's assistant switched on the light
and returned immediately to his seat.
Soon, he ran to the main entrance
asking if staff had felt or heard anything.

One section leader said she felt the walls shake.
John felt the concrete floor roll under his feet.
"What is it?" wondered others.
"Could it be a quake?" John asked.

Upon inspection the next morning,
they saw walls that had squiggles in the paint.
Anxiously, staff turned to their iPhones for news.

Shaken Up (continued)

The weather news reported an earthquake
an hour from their location, and stories of
outlying areas feeling subsequent tremors.

Roofing had blown from nearby warehouses.
Vehicles were swept into a chasm by swift water
that ruptured the main highway.

Neighborhoods lost power and trees.
While we in the West observed light damage,
the Eastern Hemisphere woke to devastation.

Few homes survived; many people were trapped,
Water was not potable, food was destroyed.
Children and pets were lost or buried in the rubble.

The Red Cross and Red Crescent awaited authorization
to enter emergency areas, to assess damages, and
to deliver cleanup supplies with food and blankets.

Other first responders were prepared
to go at a moment's notice to provide rescue and recovery.
Responders would look after their neighbors.

SET 8

Heroes

Life in America: Before and After 911
PART I

No country had declared war on America's soil
since the nineteenth century.
Late in the twentieth century, two jumbo jets attacked
the Twin Towers of the World Trade Center in New York.
It was an alarming turning point in American history.

Americans watched the attack on television.
Fear of a changing world had arrived in American homes.
Morning news anchors brought the play-by-play commentary
as hundreds of fellow citizens ran for their lives,
or jumped away from the flames.

First responders rushed to them
to evacuate those remaining in the crumbling towers
that earlier defined the city's skyline.[10]

Their only mission that day
was to help Americans escape death.
Their motivation was a shared loyalty to freedom
and a common need to keep America's promise of
life, liberty, and the pursuit of happiness.

---

[10] IMG 002.pdf "Flag Raising at Ground Zero," photographed by Thomas E. Franklin, the *Record* Newspaper. (See poems pages 80 and 81.)

Life in America: Before and After 911

PART II
ARMAGEDDON AND APOCALYPSE

Words once spoken among theologians and prophets,
folks now use Armageddon and Apocalypse
to speak of political skirmishes
or the aftermath of natural disasters.

Apocalypse, once the total disintegration of civilization,
transitioned to a special effect in movies,
not a real threat or supernatural occurrence
but a game kids play on electronic gadgets.
Shoot the villain, end the game.
Start a new game, and do it again.

Gun violence on America's streets, in American households,
at American parks, schools, and houses of worship
has brought us to a scary place.
Armageddon and the Apocalypse:
Words of future destruction and deliverance,
Promise of survival for believers,
denigrated to the colloquial,
caught in the shadow of the vernacular,
as apathy and disdain rise
in face of heroic efforts to restore a nation's hope.

Fear resides in our marrow to protect us from the formidable
and deliver us from our lesser selves.
While fear can bring positive change,
We do well to aspire to freedom from its destruction
and build a new world with hope.

Abandonment

Those who find themselves abandoned
have lost the support
of those they have loved.
Those who give themselves to complete abandon
have found the support
of One who loves them.

"If you would lose your life for my sake,
You will find it."[11]

---

[11] Holy Bible, New Revised Standard Version (Nashville: Nelson, 1990). New Testament: Gospel of Matthew 16:25. (Jesus teaching the Sermon on the Mount).

Mr. Lincoln

Larger than life, he sits atop an overstuffed chair.
Left hand in a fist, right hand poised to tap,
Booted feet set flat against the marble floor.

Head on, he has a somber, austere look.
Slightly toward his back, his person is lost,
and only his massive presence remains.
To his left side, a gentle gaze discernibly thoughtful,
pities us in our need for aggression.

Gettysburg was the Battleground
where he determined to end a brothers' war.
His inaugural claimed a president's hope for
peace beyond the battle.

How dare we tread here but lightly,
with hearts of resolve
to live past the misdeeds of makers of war
and to make peace among the human family?[12]

---

[12] The image of the Lincoln Memorial on Independence Mall in Washington DC is credited as follows on the web: Lincoln_0-43_1861.pdf

Vietnam Veterans Memorial

If I came this way daily, it would still overwhelm me:
The Names Wall of peers gone to war.
The "war that was no war," that we labeled "conflict,"
a tragic drama amid endless horror.

Vietnam became America's plumb line for justice!
It pulled at our hearts, our spirit, our common will.
We watched on TV as our soldiers endured
long, hot days in wet jungles afar.
We awaited their return in a political quagmire.
Decency within was questioned in the day's news.
Our nation's honor was tested and judged,
by a refiner's fire of justice among us.

Taste the long, flat, black wall,
etched with names of lives lost,
and see your own reflection!
Their names and ours
affixed invisibly between the lines,
beneath the friends, siblings, children, and parents
gone from the fiber of our nation,
woven into our flag and our conscience.

Our hearts still yearn for their peace and our own
as we seek sense among the ashes of our past.

David and Goliath

A young determined spirit
in good conscience and naivety
plucked a stone, set it in his sling,
hurled it toward a target,
and struck the lumbering Giant.

Goliath died.
David became King.[13]

Hope and a full heart of goodwill,
motivated toward victory o'er
brute strength and hunger for power
strengthens the humble to lead with confidence
those who would greedily control the world.

Hope could bring a revolution
a restoration of dignity
a revival of clear purpose
honoring the past, insuring the future
worthy of the genius, generosity,
and governing model of Democracy.

The grace to search for freedom
carries an equal burden of responsibility
as we seek to be creatures of goodwill.

---

[13] Holy Bible: New Revised Standard Version (Nashville: Thomas Nelson, 1990), Old Testament: I Samuel 17:38–51, pp. 261–262.

Prayer of an Itinerant Preacher

God of grace,
Lead us through this transient life
In the assurance that
You, at least,
are not temporary.

Amen.

Epilogue

When your two roads diverge in your woods,
Will you say, with Robert Frost,
you took the one less travelled?
Did it make a difference?[14]

---

[14] *American Literature and English Literature*, Revised, 1958. (New York: Harcourt, Brace & World, Inc.) Editor, Louis Untermeyer. "The Road Not Taken," Robert Frost, pp. 187–188.

Research Bibliography

The Centering Moment, Howard Thurman, (New York: Harper & Row Publishers, Inc.), 1969.

Collected Poems, 1909-1935, T.S. Eliot (New York: Harcourt, Brace & World, Inc.) 1934, 1936

The Craft of Writing, William Sloane; Julia H. Sloane, Editor (New York: W.W. Norton & Co.) Paperback 1983

Drawing on the Right Side of The Brain, A Course in Enhancing Creativity and Artistic Confidence, Revised and Expanded, Betty Edwards, (Los Angeles, CA: Jeremy P. Tarcher, Inc., St. Martin's Press, NY) 1989.

The Enlightened Heart, an Anthology of Sacred Poetry, Stephen Mitchell, Editor. (NY: Harper Collins Publishers, Inc., Perennial Edition) 1993

HAIKU, Collection of Classic Japanese Poetry selected by Mary Dawson Hughes (Kansas City, MO: Hallmark Edition, 1970 selected from Tokyo, Japan: Hokuseido Press edition, Volumes 1-4)

Holy Bible, New Revised Standard Version, (Nashville, TN: Thomas Nelson Publishers, Graded Press for Cokesbury) 1990.

The House by the Sea, A Journal, May Sarton, (New York: W.W. Norton) 1981.

The Lion and the Rose, Poems, May Sarton. (New York: Rinehart & Company, Inc.) 1948.

A Manual for Writers of Term Papers, Theses, and Dissertations, Kate L. Turabian, F*ifth Edition; Revised and Expanded by Bonnie Birtwistle Honigsblum* (Chicago, IL: University of Chicago Press) 1987.

Modern American Poetry and Modern British Poetry, Louis Untermeyer, Editor. (NY: Harcourt, Brace & World, Inc.) 1958 and 1962.

On the Pulse of Morning, the Inaugural Poem, Maya Angelou: (New York: Random House, Inc), 1993.

The Oxford Book of English Verse, 1250–1918 Sir Arthur Quiller-Couch, Editor (New York: Oxford University Press) 1940. (First published, 1900) Anthology of 13th through 19th Century Poetry.

Poems, Maya Angelou, Includes "Just Give Me a Cool Drink of Water "fore I Diiie," "Oh Pray My Wings Are Gonna Fit Me Well," "And Still I Rise": (New York: Random House, Inc., Bantom Books) 1981.

The Record newspaper (Bergen County Record, Passaic, N.J.) *Flag Raising at Ground Zero* [911] IMG-002.jpg Photo: Thomas E. Franklin, NJ 2011 [Retrieved from Website 11/14/19] www.Loc.gov/rr/print/res/306_fran.html.

Recovering, A Journal, May Sarton. (New York: W.W. Norton and Company) Paperback 1986.

Roget's International Thesaurus, Robert L. Chapman revision: 4th Edition (London: Harper and Row, Publishers) 1979.

Sabbaths, Wendell Berry (New York: Farrar, Straus and Giroux/North Point Press Division) 1995 Printing

Spiritual Marketplace, Baby Boomers and the Remaking of American Religion, Wade Clark Roof (Princeton, N.J.: Princeton University Press) 3rd printing, 2001

A Testament of Devotion, Thomas R. Kelley; *With a Biographical Memoir by Douglas V. Steere* (New York: Harper & Row Publishers) 1941, pp. 1–28

www.jweekly.com/2018/03/29/foldable-israeli-car-s-f-parking-woes, Maya Mirsky [Jewish News of Northern California] Courtesy of City Transformer. 2018.

Wouldn't Take Nothing for My Journey Now, Maya Angelou (New York: Random House) 1993.

Writing the Natural Way, A *Course in Enhancing Creativity and Writing Confidence,* Gabriele Lusser Rico, (Los Angeles, CA: J. P. Tarcher, Inc., Houghton Mifflin Company, Boston) 1983.

Historical Influence in Poetry's Development

Old English Influences in Poetry

Geoffrey Chaucer, *The Canterbury Tales,* Nevill Coghill, Translator (Baltimore: Penguin Books, Inc., 1952) Revision reprint: 1963. (First Edition: 1888 Oxford).

- Introduction to Chaucer's life and works, including how he was drawn to poetry and the life experiences that encouraged his writing.
- Fourteenth-century English history and culture in which the literature grew.
- European influences on Chaucer and his writing help to explain the content of his poetry.
- The importance of reading widely to the developing poet.
- The place of languages in the poet's knowledge.
- The need for patrons and sponsors for writers and artists in Chaucer's time.
- Referral to additional resources:
- *The Poet Chaucer* in the Home University Library series, by Nevill Coghill

Latin and Greek Influences in Poetry

Select Poems of Catullus, Edited with English Introductions, Notes and Appendices by Francis P. Simpson, Balliol College, Oxford; London: MacMillan & Co. LTD; New York: St. Martin's Press, 1961. (First Edition: 1879)

The Latin poet, Catullus, was almost extinct before he could be properly introduced to the public. His main work, a manuscript of his diary, was rescued from the destruction of Rome as Imperialism became prominent there.

Two outstanding Greek poets of the first century BC were Virgil and Ovid. Their most prominent works are Virgil's *Aeneid* and *Metamorpheses* by Ovid. These works represent a major preference exemplified by Augustus Caesar for poetry.

Journal Writing and Poetry

May Sarton, *At Seventy: The Journals of May Sarton* (New York: W.W. Norton & Co., copyright 1984; reissued, 1993).